I0606118

Corrie ten Boom

Are all of the watches safe?

The true story of Corrie ten Boom and the little Dutch watch shop

Catherine Mackenzie
Illustrated by Rita Ammassari

Corrie ten Boom lived in a little watch shop in the middle of Holland. She lived there with her papa, mama, and her sister Betsie. It was a pretty little shop, with a sign by the door. The window was full of watches that ticked away gently. In the background the clocks made loud ringing noises.

Corrie ten Boom lived in a little watch shop in the middle of Holland.

Corrie loved her papa. He was one of the best watchmakers in the city. Corrie's papa loved God and he loved to teach his little girls about him too. Corrie felt safe with her papa. She felt even safer when she knew that God loved her. It was wonderful to know that loving and trusting in Jesus was all she needed to do. Jesus' love would keep her safe forever – even when she died. Corrie had never felt so safe before.

Corrie felt safe with her papa.
She felt even safer when she knew
that God loved her.

Corrie wanted to be a watchmaker like her papa. When she passed her watchmaker's exams, Corrie's family had a big celebration. Corrie was so pleased. She loved working in the shop and every evening she made sure that the doors were locked. 'Are all of the watches safe?' Corrie muttered as she checked the locks. 'Everything's safe Corrie,' said Papa. 'It's time to eat.'

Every evening Corrie made sure that the doors were locked.

One day Corrie and Betsie woke up to the sound of aeroplanes flying overhead. They ran to the window and looked out.

Enemy planes covered the sky. The Nazis had invaded Holland. Their country was at war. Bombs were dropped from the sky, day and night, until Holland was defeated.

Enemy planes covered the sky.

Corrie did all she could to help people escape from the enemy. Corrie would cycle through the city to pass on secret messages. Jewish people were in lots of danger. Many of them were put in prison.

'We must help these poor people,' Corrie gasped. 'They need somewhere to hide.' But where would they find a safe place?

Corrie would cycle through the city to pass on secret messages.

That was when Corrie's room was made into a hiding place. A special secret room was added onto the end of her bedroom. Anybody who needed a place to hide could come and stay with the ten Boom family.

When the enemy came, Corrie and Betsie would hide the people in the secret room until the soldiers went away. When the danger was over Corrie would whisper a prayer of thanks to God. 'Everyone's safe God. Thank you. Thank you so much.'

When the enemy came, Corrie and Betsie would hide the people in the secret room.

However, one day the enemy found out that Corrie's family were helping Jews escape. Nazi guards came to the watch shop and hammered on the door. Corrie's friends hid inside the secret room. They got in just in time. A Nazi guard marched into the watch shop and took Corrie away. It was her turn to go to prison now.

It was a horrible and frightening day, but as she left in the back of an army truck, Corrie thanked God that the Nazis had not found the secret room. Her friends were safe for now.

Corrie's *family* were helping
Jews escape.

The prison was a horrible place to be. Corrie was all alone. Her family were in prison too, but she was not allowed to see them. She was tired and hungry and very sad.

When she heard that her papa had died, Corrie's eyes filled with tears. But she knew that he had gone home to be with Jesus.

'That's what heaven is like,' she thought. 'It's just like going home. Papa is safe. Nobody can hurt him now. He is with Jesus.'

The prison was a horrible place to be.
Corrie was all alone.

Corrie was surprised one morning when a parcel arrived for her. 'Why is the address written so strangely? It's almost as if they want me to look at the stamp. Perhaps they do?' Corrie gasped. Quietly she peeled the stamp away. Underneath was a secret message, 'All of the watches are safe.'

Corrie smiled. It was a secret message to tell her that the people in the secret room had escaped. 'Thank you, Jesus,' Corrie whispered. 'Thank you for keeping them safe.'

‘Thank you, Jesus,’ Corrie whispered.

Corrie spent many months in different prisons. One of these prisons was called Ravensbruck. For some of that time she was with her sister Betsie, but when Betsie died, Corrie was on her own.

However, Corrie knew that God was with her. Even if she died, God would keep her safe. Corrie knew that there is no place safer than heaven.

Corrie spent many months in different prisons.

Then an amazing thing happened. An enemy guard made a mistake and Corrie was set free. Soon afterwards the war ended.

Corrie remembered the watches and the secret room and how God always keeps his people safe.

'So many people need to know that the only way to be really safe is to trust in Jesus Christ,' Corrie thought.

'Jesus died for me. That is what I will tell the world,' Corrie said. 'Trusting in Jesus and what he did is the only way to be truly safe.'

Corrie said, 'Trusting in Jesus is the only way to be truly safe.'

For Lydia, Esther, Lois, Marianne, Isobel and Elizabeth
With love and prayers that you too will be safe
with the Lord Jesus.

Reprinted 2008, 2011, 2014, 2016, 2019, 2020, 2022,
2023 and 2025
ISBN: 978-1-84550-109-9

Published by Christian Focus Publications
Geanies House, Fearn, Tain, Ross-shire, IV20 1TW,
Scotland, U.K. www.christianfocus.com

Cover design by Daniel van Straaten
Illustrated by Rita Ammassari
Printed and bound by Imprint, India